TURPIN'S RIDE TO YORK;

OR, BONNY BLACK BESS.

AN EQUESTRIAN DRAMA, IN TWO ACTS.

BY H. M. MILNER.

First performed at Astley's Amphitheatre, on Whit Monday, 1836.

Dramatis Personæ.

[See page 7.

SIR RANALPH ROOKWOOD	Mr. Widdicomb.
DICK TURPIN (the celebrated highwayman)	Mr. W. Elliott.
TOM KING (the gentleman highwayman)	Mr. S. Palmer.
SIMON SHARPSCENT (a special constable and beadle of Westminster)	Mr. S. Smith.
SAM SHARPSCENT (his son, an attorney)	Mr. Fillingham.
TIMOTHY GUDGEON (a fishmonger)	Mr. C. Marshall.
RALPH (ostler at Stamford)	Mr. J. George.
RUST	Mr. W. Taylor.
SWIFT } (Essex gang)	Mr. H. Widdicomb.
ROSE	Mr. King.

No. 632. Dicks' Standard Plays.

CONTINUATION OF DRAMATIS PERSONÆ.

DOLLY GUDGEON ... ... Miss Goward.
ELEANOR ... ... Mrs. Stickney.
MRS. PODGER (widow and landlady of The Yorkshire Grey) ... ... Mrs. Lawrence.
SUSAN FIELDER ... ... Miss Enscoe.

GIPSY TRIBE.

LUKE ROOKWOOD (the gipsy heir) ... ... Mr. Cartlitch.
BALTHAZAR (patrico of the tribe) ... ... Mr. B. Rayner.
BARBARA LOVELL (the mystic hag of the tribe) ... ... Madame Simon.
SYBIL (her daughter) ... ... Mrs. Pope.

TIME OF REPRESENTATION.—One Hour and Thirty Minutes.

COSTUME.

TURPIN.—Green riding frock, trimmed with gold braid—long green waistcoat, leather breeches, yellow top riding-boots, white cravat, gold laced hat, spurs.

KING.—Drab great coat over a red hunting coat—waistcoat and white cord breeches—riding-boots, gold-laced hat and powdered wig, spurs and riding-whip.

SIR RANALPH.—Black square-cut coat, breeches trimmed with gold lace, lace neckcloth and ruffles.

SIMON SHARPSCENT.—Beadle's coat with cape—top-boots, Midas wig.

SAM SHARPSCENT.—Square cut fustian coat and breeches, red waistcoat, top-boots, three-cornered hat, club wig with tail.

TIMOTHY GUDGEON.—Cut off blue coat, light waistcoat and breeches, sugar-loaf hat, pumps, and striped stockings.

RALPH.—Short smock frock, leather breeches, grey stockings, half boots, red hair.

RUST, SWIFT, ROSE.—Square-cut coats, and breeches of brown, grey, puce and drab, jack-boots, square-toed shoes, buckles, &c.

LUKE ROOKWOOD.—Dark brown square-cut coat, patched, and breeches, grey worsted stockings, darned, red handkerchief, three-cornered hat.

BALTHAZAR.—Dark russet doublet and trunks, flat brimmed hat, flesh leggings, staff in hand.

DOLLY GUDGEON.—Chintz tuck-up dress, mits, circular straw hat, with silk ribbons.

ELEANOR.—Slate coloured silk, open gown, with short sleeves, trimmed with lace, white petticoat, hair dishevelled.

SUSAN FIELDER.—Riding habit, hat and feather.

BARBARA.—Long red gown, patched, with turban head-dress.

SYBIL.—Red petticoat, black velvet body, ringlets, scarf, &c.

GIPSIES.—Motley ragged costumes.

STAGE DIRECTIONS.

EXITS AND ENTRANCES.—R. means *Right*; L. *Left*; D. F. *Door in Flat*; R. D. *Right Door*; L. D. *Left Door*; S. E. *Second Entrance*; U. E. *Upper Entrance*; M. D. *Middle Door*; L. U. E. *Left Upper Entrance*; R. U. E. *Right Upper Entrance*; L. S. E. *Left Second Entrance*; P. S. *Prompt Side*; O. P. *Opposite Prompt*.

RELATIVE POSITIONS.—R. means *Right*; L. *Left*; C. *Centre*; R. C. *Right of Centre*; L. C., *Left of Centre*.

R.   RC.   C.   LC.   L.

₊ *The Reader is supposed to be on the Stage, facing the Audience.*

TURPIN'S RIDE TO YORK.

ACT I.

SCENE I.—*Gipsies' encampment in the vaults of Rookwood Priory.* BARBARA, SYBIL, BALTHAZAR, *and gipsy tinkers, &c., discovered sitting around a fire,* c.

Bal. This stray capon will yield us a rare repast to-night. What can delay Luke Bradley? His dark-eyed beauty, the pretty Sybil, can tell us—hath heard of him to-day?

Syb. I have. (*Sighs.*) Heigho!

Bar. I see—a lovers' quarrel. Old as I am, I've not forgot my feelings as a girl. Luke has a surly temper, is it not so?

Syb. This is no lovers' quarrel, at once to be forgotten and forgiven. Would it were so!

Bar. What is it, then? hath he betrayed thee? tell me, girl, in what way, that I may avenge thee? If it be thy wrongs require revenge, he shall wed thee within this hour, if thou wilt! My power is not yet departed.

Syb. Mother, he hath not injured me; he cannot help it!

Bar. Help what?

Syb. Sir Pierre is dead.

Bar. Dead! Sir Pierre dead?

Syb. And Luke Bradley——

Bar. Ha!

Syb. Is his successor.

Bar. Who told thee that?

Syb. Luke himself; I know all—all is discovered. He is now Sir Luke Rookwood!

Bar. This is news, in truth, yet not news to weep for. Thou shouldst rejoice, not lament. I knew it—I shall live to see all accomplished, to see her wedded. Sybil, thou shalt be Lady Rookwood!

Syb. Never—it cannot be!

Bar. Not be! Why should it not be? Ha! the truth flashes on me—he hath discarded thee!

Syb. No, he is still unaltered in affection; but, mother, it is not fitting that a gipsy girl should mate with him.

Bar. Not fitting! Get up, or I will spurn thee! Not fitting! Dry thine eyes, or I will stab thee! Thou shalt have a dower as ample as that of any lady in the land!

Syb. If I wed, a curse will light upon me.

Bar. Leave that to me. I was present at his mother's death.

Syb. Was there a ring upon her finger?

Bar. There was—a wedding-ring.

Syb. Then they are wedded, and Luke is the rightful heir!

Bar. I have the proof, the solemn attestation of his rights. Behold this withered hand, I took it from the shrouded corpse of his mother, Susan Bradley; see thou this ring glistening upon her finger? It was placed there by Sir Pierre. The hand that bears it was joined to him at the altar, before his faith was plighted to his present wife. Years have passed since this ring was placed upon her finger. I would have told Luke long, long ago, had not an oath sealed my lips.

Syb. How did she die?

Bar. She was smothered, sleeping. I was sent for by Sir Pierre; I saw before me her murderer—he trembled as I looked upon him. "You were her assassin! there is a ring upon her finger; she was your wife." "She was," he cried, in agony, "give me up to justice." I took an oath never to divulge the secret during his life-time. He led me into another chamber, where lay a sleeping boy; it was Luke! "Take this child," cried he," or the sight of it will madden me." Years passed away, and Luke is the boldest of our tribe. I've affianced you. He is Sir Luke; he is your husband.

Syb. Hold, mother! he is not yet Sir Luke Rookwood, and it hath been said, that if Rook mate not with Rook, their possessions shall pass away. Thou shalt hear the prophecy :—

When the stray rook shall perch on the topmost
        bough,
There shall be clamour and screeching, I trow;
But of right to, and rule of, the ancient nest,
The rook that with rook mates, shall be possessed.

Bal. Luke is the stray rook, and this new-found cousin is the rook that must mate with a rook, or relinquish her and the ancient creed to his brother, by the present Lady Rookwood.

Bar. Is he not in our power, confined in yonder cell?   (*Whistle without.*)

Bal. Hark! 'tis Luke's signal!

Music.—LUKE *enters,* L. H. U. E., *bearing* ELEANOR, *insensible, in his arms.*

Luke. I am pursued—guard the entrance! Sybil, this maiden requires your aid.

Bar. You have been to Sir Pierre's funeral?

Luke. I have; but not to gaze upon the vain and idle mockery of a funeral pageant; nobler motives drew me thither. My new-found cousin, you beauteous fair one, was the cause of my visit there. Eleanor Mowbray is the heiress to the lands of Rookwood. They were bequeathed to her by the hand of Sir Reginald—or, rather, to the female issue, and such is she. By making her my bride I shall hold possession; the certificate of my mother's marriage is only wanting to prove my claim to Rookwood's vast domains.

Bar. (*Crossing.*) Thy bride, liar! There is thy bride!   (*Pointing to Sybil.*)

Luke. The fates have willed it otherwise. I have sworn she shall be mine, and no power on earth shall prevent it. This very hour shall the rites be performed, even in the vaults of Rookwood!

Bar. Make not too sure of that. Eleanor Mowbray shall never become the wife of one of our tribe!

Ele. (*Recovering.*) Where am I?

Luke. In safety—with friends and your future husband.

Ele. My husband? Never! Death sooner!

Luke. This will not avail. Mine you must and shall be! Proceed with the ceremony.

WEDDING CHORUS OF GIPSIES.

Scrape the catgut, pass the liquor,
Let your swift feet move the quicker—
    Ta, ra, la!
Dance and sing in jolly chorus,
Bride and bridegroom are before us,
And the patriarch stands o'er us—
    Ta, ra, la!

(*Grand mock inauguration and gipsy wedding, during which* RANALPH *appears at the grating,* R. *He fires a pistol at the crowd.*)

Ran. Hold, ruffians! I have the power——

Luke. Thy power I scorn, and heed not thy words! Beware lest I become a fratricide!

Ran. Fratricide!

Luke. Ranalph Rookwood, the name you bear is mine, and by a right as good as yours. I am your elder brother, and you are in my power.

Bal. (*Rushes down,* L.) The constables have discovered our secret entrance, and hasten hither to liberate Sir Ranalph.

(*The Constables, rushing in,* L. H., *release Sir Ranalph. Terrific encounter between officers and gipsies. During the fight, Sybil and Barbara hurry Eleanor off,* 1 E. R. *Sam Sharpscent is knocked down by Balthazar.*)

Sam. Oh, father, here's a go! They have been and made a large hole in my crown the size of a five-shilling piece.

Luke. (c., *Over the prostrate body of Sir Ranalph, with uplifted weapon.*) This would end all; but you are my brother.

(*Tableau.—Scene closes.*)

SCENE II.—*Interior of the "Yorkshire Grey."—Music.—Gate-bell heard without.*

Enter LANDLADY, R, *calling.*

Land. Here, John, Ralph, you lazy dogs! Here's company coming, and no room ready. (*Places tables and chairs, opens the door,* L. C., *and ushers in* TOM KING *and Highwaymen.*) This way, gentlemen. Ah! it's a brave band formed by you gentlemen of the road. Lone widow that I am, since my last husband's sudden death at Tyburn, I don't know what would have become of me but for your charitable visits.   (*Sighs.*)

King. No more sighing about your husband, hostess; recollect sudden death is what we are all subject to. Come, lads, a stirrup cup at parting, and then hurrah for the game of high toby!

(*Gate-bell rings.*)

Hostess. (*Looking through window.*) Gentlemen, there's a chaise just arrived, and this is the only room vacant. Will you mind them coming in here?

King. Oh, no! Show them in, by all means.

TIMOTHY GUDGEON, *a' Cockney, appears at window.*

Tim. I say, landlady, I sees written up outside, "Good accommodation for man and beast." What do you charge for a pint of fourpenny and an 'oss's bait?

Host. Why, to a gentleman, twopence the ale and fourpence the bait.

Tim. That's twopence more than I pays in London.

Host. Well, then, twopence halfpenny won't hurt you.

Tim. Well, as it is a very warm day, I don't mind patronizing you, so send your ostler round to take care of my 'oss.   [*Exits.*

King. These yokels are worth diving into, and, thanks to my toggery, I can queer these brother blades of the road.

(*Pointing to the highwaymen seated at table.*)

Music.—TIMOTHY *and* DOLLY *enter,* D. L. C.

Tim. Come along, my dear; make haste with that pint of ale.

King. And bring me a pint of wine.

Dol. La, Timothy! I thought you said there was no one here. Why, there is no chair to sit down upon.

King. (*Advancing.*) Mine, madam, is at your service.

Dol. Oh, how very polite! May I, Timothy?

(*She curtsies, and upsets Timothy, who rises in a rage.*)

Tim. I say, where are you shoving to? You go there, then I have my eye upon you—safe bind, safe find.   (*Places his riding-box by his side.*)

HOSTESS *enters with wine and ale.*

Host. Here's your wine, sir. (*Crosses to Timothy.*) Here's your ale.   (*Gruffly.*)

King. (*Presenting glass of wine to Dolly.*) Perhaps a glass of wine will be preferable?

Dol. May I, Timothy?

Tim. Of course; never refuse anything that is offered to you.

Dol. Let us hob and nob, Timothy.

King. You have been riding?

Dol. Yes, sir; we have come a matter of ten miles—three more will bring us to our journey's end. We are going to Mr. Saunders—perhaps you know him, sir?

Tim. Yes, sir; we are going to Mr. Saunders'. She was a Miss Saunders—now she's my wife. Very pretty, ain't she?

King. Pretty! Extremely handsome—a perfect angel!

Dol. La! Timothy, don't go on in that way, you make me blush all over like a cauliflower.

King. (*Aside.*) A red cabbage she means; it's time to see if these pigeons are worth the plucking. (*Aloud.*) Hostess, take the reckoning and bring me the change out of this fifty pound note.

Host. Sorry to say I've not so much in the house by forty-nine pounds nineteen shillings and elevenpence three farthings.

King. Damn your three farthings! Then you must trust me.

Host. (*Aside.*) Yes, but not out of sight.

Dol. Law, Timothy, why don't you oblige the gentleman? You have got lots of gold in your riding-box.

Tim. (*Aside.*) Be quiet. How could you be so foolish?

King. I find I've sufficient to pay the bill. (*Pays.*) Another glass of wine, and——

Dol. Your bottle will be empty.

King. (*Aside.*) So will your riding-box before I've done.

Tim. (*Rising and crossing to Hostess.*) Just see if my 'oss is done; if so, put her to. Meanwhile, I'll amuse myself with the paper.

(*Returns to seat himself, but falls. King has taken the chair away and is seated by Dolly's side.*)

Tim. (*Coming between them.*) When that's out of hand, I'll trouble you. Remember, this is my wife; you're getting too familiar, so drop it.

King. I beg pardon, I was merely describing the country.

Tim. I can do all that for my wife myself.

Dol. How jealous you are! Now do, there's a dear, read it out.

Tim. Why, of course I should read it out if I was not at home.

Dol. Well, then, let me read it over your shoulder.

Tim. Oh! here's an account of a daring robbery committed last night.

[*Music.—While the couple are intently reading, King opens the riding-box, takes out the money and exits.*]

Tim. (*Reading the newspaper.*) Did you ever? Right before their very eyes! What a bare-faced robber!

Host. (*Entering.*) Your chaise is ready, sir.

Tim. Come along, Dolly. I'll pay you outside. I defy any one to rob me. Only to think! right before their very eyes.

(*Music.—Exeunt. The Hostess clears the stage.*)

SCENE III.—*The exterior of the rendezvous at Kilburn* RUST, SWIFT, *and* ROSE, *discovered drinking*, R. H.

Enter TOM KING, R. H.

King. That was a rare joke, and will just enable me to pay my tailor's bill. (*Bell heard without.*) Ah! the traps; I must be cautious.

(*Steps aside as the* BEADLE *enters, who is followed by* SAM SHARPSCENT *and Crowd*, R. H. U. E.

Simon. Silence! Oh, yes! This is to give notice that I am the beadle and chief constable of Westminster. (*To Sam.*) Ring the bell. This is to give notice, that last night, at eight o'clock, in the City of Westminster, a beautiful black mare was stolen; whoever will restore the same shall be rewarded. The aforesaid mare can be easily recognised, as she has been curtailed of her fair proportions—that is to say, some malicious person or persons did, on Saturday night last, cut her beautiful black glossy tail from off her body. Therefore the party or parties who did commit the aforesaid robbery must sell her wholesale, for they cannot retail her. Ring the bell. This is also to give notice that a reward of five hundred pounds is offered for the capture of that notorious highwayman, Dick Turpin. Ring the bell. And also a further reward of two hundred pounds for the apprehension of his pal the gentleman highwayman, Tom King. Ring the bell. And, lastly, this is to give notice, I've nothing more to say.

(*Music. — They go off shouting,* L. H. U. E.

King. So far, so good. Turpin must know this What can delay him with such a mare as Black Bess! Hark! I hear her hoofs! Hurrah! 'tis he.

Music.—TURPIN *rides on* R. H.

Tur. Talk of the devil and he's close at your heels. Tom, my boy, tip me your daddle, for I'm right glad to see you.

King. (*Approaching Turpin.*) Never before did highwayman possess——

For ease, security, danger, or distress,
Such a mare as Turpin's Black Bess.

Essex Gang. (*At table,* U. E. L. H.) Hear, hear! Ha! ha!

[*They rise and exeunt,* L. H. U. E.

Tur. Now we have met, we must have a bumper. Here, landlord, house! My dear Tom, you are aware that my errand to town is accomplished. I have smashed Lawyer Coate's screen, pocketed the dummock—here it is, (*Slapping his pocket.*) and, with a cool thousand in hand, I shall start for Yorkshire to-night.

King. Indeed—so soon?

Tur. To tell you the truth, I want to see how matters stand with Luke Rookwood. I should be sorry if he went to the wall for want of assistance.

King. I shall not be able to accompany you; my horse had the misfortune to get a pebble in her shoe, which will take the farrier a good half-day to extricate.

Tur. In that case, I must be off alone. But with respect to Luke Rookwood, no wonder he's in trouble. When a man once pins himself to the petticoats, it's all up with him; and, not content with one, he needs must indulge in three. There's the Lady Rookwood, his cousin Eleanor Mowbray, and the pretty, black-eyed Sybil. Now, for my part, I——

King. All you can say won't alter my good opinion of the sex. No secret have I from the girl of my heart. She could have sold me over and over again if she had chosen; but my sweet Sue is not the wench to do that.

Tur. It is not too late; your Delilah may yet hand you over to the Philistines.

King. Then I shall die in a good cause, but——

Tyburn tree
Has no terror for me.
Let better men swing—
I'm at liberty.

I shall never come to the scragging-post, unless you turn topsman. Dick, my nativity has been cast, and the stars have declared that I am to die by the hand of my best friend, and that's you.

Tur. Then it must be on terra firma, for if once you mount, I can be of service to you no longer.

[*Music.—They retire to the table and drink.*

King. And now, Dick, to change the subject; so you are off to Yorkshire to-night. 'Pon my soul, you're a wonderful fellow—an *alibi* personified—here and everywhere at the same time. No wonder you are called the Flying Highwayman—to-day in town, to-morrow in York, the day after, Chester; the devil only knows where you will pitch your quarters a week hence. There are rumours of you in all counties at the same moment. This man swears you robbed him at Hounslow—that on Salisbury Plain; while another avers you monopolize Cheshire and Yorkshire, and that it is not safe even to hunt without pops in your pocket. I heard some devilish good stories of you the other day; the fellow who told them to me little thought I was a brother blade.

Tur. You flatter me, but it is no merit of mine, Black Bess alone enables me to do it, and hers be the credit. Ah! if your mistress is only as true to you as my nag is to me, you might set at nought the tightest hempen cravat that was ever twisted :—

Let the lover his mistress's beauty rehearse,
And laud her attractions in languishing verse;
Be it mine, in rude strains but with truth, to express,
The love that I bear to my bonny Black Bess.

Look, look! how that eyeball glows bright as a brand,
That neck proudly arches, those nostrils expand.
Mark that wide flowing mane, of which each silky tress,
Might adorn prouder beauties, tho' none like Black Bess

Mark that skin, sleek as velvet and dusky as night,
With it's jet undisfigured by one spot of white;
That throat branched with veins, prompt to charge or caress.
Now, is she not beautiful? Bonny Black Bess!

King. Egad! I should say so; you are as sentimental on the subject of your mare as I am when I think of my darling Susan.

Tur. Now to business. I'm going to propose a plan rather out of our way, but still the shiners are to be got by it, and what care we? One Timothy Gudgeon——

King. What, the fishmonger? I encountered him not long since; he enabled me to pay my tailor's bill.

Tur. I am glad to hear it. But, to return to my plan—I have found, from very good authority, that he has had left him a legacy of five hundred pounds, and his wife, frightened of us gentlemen of the road, for security has sewed the money up in the bolster of her bed. They are out visiting one Mr. Saunders, so we have no fear of being surprised; besides, I've bribed the ostler here, to take the lynch-pin out; the delay occasioned by the accident will give us longer time. What say you to the trip?

King. With all my heart. I admire the plan, and am ready to set out at once. I will hire a hack of the landlord here.

Tur. That's right. The money's ours—then hey for Yorkshire!

Now for Fishmongers' Hall,
Tim Gudgeon to press—
Tom King on a hack,
And Dick Turpin on Bess.

[*The hack is brought; they mount and ride off.—Music.*

SCENE IV.—*Outside of the Fishmonger's house, in Cripplegate—Night.*

SIMON SHARPSCENT *enters, carrying a lantern, followed by his son* SAM.

Sim. I tell you, you must do it; so come along. Timothy Gudgeon said to me this morning, "I am going to take my wife to see her father, so I shall want my house guarded during my absence." He will pay handsomely for so doing.

Sam. I don't see why I should do it, for you gets the browns, and I gets all the work.

Sim. Well, there's a shilling for you. Now are you satisfied?   (*Gives one.*)

Sam. Why, what's a shilling for watching all night in the cold? I must have something to drink as well.

Sim. I am afraid, Sam, you are addicted to drinking. Well, this once I don't mind doing the liberal; so come with me to the next street, and I will call for a half-pint of half-and-half, and have the first swig at it.

[*Exeunt.*

TOM KING *and* TURPIN *enter.*

Tur. This is the house. Look out!

[*Music.—Turpin picks the lock; they enter the house by the door, which they close after them.*

TIMOTHY *and* DOLLY *enter, covered with mud,* L.

Tim. Only to think of the wheel coming off the chaise just as we got into London! Here's a pickle I'm in!

Dol. Yes; but your wife's preserved—that's one consolation.

Tim. Then take the key, and open the door.

Dol. You make me do all the work—I'm a perfect slave, that I am.

Tim. Then why didn't you marry the butcher?

Dol. I wish I did.

Tim. So do I, for he would have killed you by this time; what a fuss you make about nothing! Now suppose our money had gone, then you would have cause to complain.

Dol. You have to thank me for proposing to hide it in the bolster, and the few friends of mine that I happened to mention it to, said——

Tim. Oh, you have told your friends, have you?

Dol. Yes; only half-a-dozen of my most particular friends, whom I can trust.

Tim. Well, if they are women, it's all over the town by this time; so come along in, Mrs. Gudgeon, or we shall take cold.

[*They enter the house.*

SCENE V.—*The Bedroom.*

The THIEVES *discovered.*

King. We had better depart at once while the coast is clear.

Timothy. (*Outside.*) Come along, Dolly.

King. Hark! they have come home. This shall quiet them.

Tur. No, no; we can escape without committing murder, for that is a crime that makes the stoutest heart tremble.

(*They conceal themselves as* DOLLY *and* TIMOTHY *enter.*)

Tim. Suppose we go to bed at once without supper; we shall rise in the morning with a better appetite.

Dol. Well, we can't go to bed in the dark. I left a candle on the table.

(*She lights it by means of the lantern. Turpin crawls from under the table, and blows both out.*)

Tim. There you are, at your larks again. I've a great mind to put you out, and let you sleep in the cold all night.

Dol. You needn't be so cross. You will find the matches in the cupboard, goose.

Tim. Well, ducky. I didn't know I had a match there.

King. (*Aside, as Timothy opens the cupboard.*) Yes, there's his match.

(*King passes from the cupboard by crawling through Timothy's legs.*)

Dol. I shall take off my thingamies, and get into bed.

(*As she retires towards the bed, she encounters King's leg.*)

There's that Tom cat always in the way; whist! cat!

(*Goes into the bed-room, discovers Turpin; she screams and calls "Murder—thieves!" King and Turpin tie them together with the sheets as the scene closes.*)

SCENE VI.—*Same as Scene IV.*—*The* CONSTABLE *enters, followed by his* SON, R. H.

Sam. Oh, father! I'm sure there's a row. Someone's calling for help.

Sim. Oh, if that's the case, I'll knock them all down, and take them all up.

(*Music—They go to the fishmonger's door, and knock loudly. The window above opens. Turpin and King descend, carrying a box, which they drop in effecting their escape. Simon springs his rattle. OFFICERS enter R., DOLLY runs on calling "Murder." TIM enters with blunderbuss, he fires; in the scuffle Tim falls over the box; the watchman, seeing him with it, seize and drag him off, L., supposing him to be the thief; Dolly in hysterics.*)

SCENE VII.—*Exterior of a public-house, same as Scene III.*, KING *and* TURPIN *gallop on,* R. H. *Music.*)

Tur. Only to think, Tom, of robbing the same man twice in one day. But we must lose no time, rip the bolster open, we'll divide the swag fairly. Quick! for our pursuers are close upon us.

King. This is all through me. Why not have left me upon the road? For, with the swiftness of Bess, the devil's in it if you couldn't have given them the go-by.

(*Music.* SIMON SHARPSCENT, *and his son* SAM, *arm-in-arm with* SUSAN FIELDER (*King's mistress*), *followed by officers, enter at the back,* R. H. *Susan identifies the highwayman. Officers rush down—a struggle ensues—King is captured,* L. H.)

King. Fire, Dick, or I'm taken! Damn it, why don't you fire? (*Struggling.*)

Tur. I shall hit you if I do.

King. Take your chance! Is this your friendship?

Tur. Deserting a friend in the hour of distress, Is never the maxim of Turpin or Bess!

(*Turpin fires; the ball strikes King by mistake, who drops wounded.*)

King. Susan, is it you? Did she betray me? Oh, perfidious woman! My best friend, Turpin—— I die by his hand! (*Falls dead,* C.)

Tur. Damn the popper! We must be off to Yorkshire now, and by hell we'll do it, and the devil take the hindmost. (*Music.*)

Omnes. Turpin! After him!

(*General pursuit. Turpin, in his haste, upsets a donkey-cart heavily laden with vegetables. The mob pelt the pursuers.*)

END OF ACT I.

ACT II.

SCENE I.—*Outside of the Hornsey Toll-gate,* L. H. *Music. Clock strikes ten. The* GATEKEEPER *enters,* D. F. L. H.

Keep. Ten o'clock! Well, I've made a pretty day's work of it. Two pounds for myself, and one pound for the Commissioners. What a thing it is to have an honest man like myself on the trust. There will be nothing through till the York mail passes in the morning, so I can shut the gate for the night, and turn in for a snooze. If anyone wants to go through, they must wait my convenience.

(*Music.—Locks the gate, and goes in.* TURPIN *gallops on,* R. H.)

Tur. Confusion! the gate is closed, and that rascally keeper fast asleep. My pursuers close to my heels, too. No matter! Bess, my girl, you have never failed me at a pinch, nor will you now. We know a way, don't we, wench? by which we can save the pence as well. So up, wench, and over.

(*Leaps gate, pursuers enter, the* GATEKEEPER *comes out.*)

Sim. Open the gate, fellow, and quickly! Don't you see the notorious highwayman, Turpin, has escaped us?

Keep. Lord bless us! There he goes, sure enough.

(*Holding up his lantern, and looking off in the direction.*)

Sim. Open the gate, fellow, and be expeditious!

Keep. Not I, unless I get my dues. I have been done once already; strike me stupid if I be done a second time.

Sim. Don't you perceive that I am Chief Constable of Westminster?

Keep. That may be; but you don't pass unless I get the blunt.

Sim. (*Gives money.*) Here, you scoundrel!

Keep. Why, it's a bad sixpence!

Sim. Don't you see he'll gain ground through this delay?

Keep. Now don't flurry yourself in this way; see how quietly I takes it. Oh, bless me, here's a precious go! I've lost the key of the gate. (*Looks about for it, after feeling in all his pockets.*) Oh, here it is; now there's something in the keyhole!

Sim. I will report this case, you may depend.
(*Rushes through gate. Keeper stays his Son.*)

Keep. Well, and where are you going?

Sam. Why, after Turpin, to be sure. So open the gate, or I shall ride over you.

Keep. I am very sorry, but you don't go through this gate unless you tips.

Sam. Why, my father paid for me.

Keep. Was that rum old chap your father?

Sam. Yes, that was my venerable parent.

Keep. Well, all I can say is that unless you walks out the brads you can't go any farther with your father.

Sam. (*Calling.*) Father! Come back and lend me twopence.

Simon. (*Without.*) I can't—I'm in a ditch!

Keep. It's of no use, so you must pay.

Sam. How can I pay when I ain't got no money?

Keep. Well, then, you must leave your boots.

Sam. I never heard of such a thing; how can I ride without my boots?

Keep. Well, I don't think you can ride with them.

Sam. Here, take my breast pin.

Keep. It ain't worth anything.
(*Examining it.*)

Sam. Oh! ain't it, though? It's real Brummagum; I gave one shilling and sixpence for it last week in the New Cut.

Keep. I suppose I must let you through.
[*Exit Sam.*
(TINKER *follows on donkey, with bunch of carrots in front.*)

Keep. And where are you going?

Tin. Why, to catch Turpin, to be sure, so you had better open the gate at once, for I know my Billy's temper, and I can't hold him in much longer.

Keep. But you must pay, my tulip.

Tin. Well, take my riding-whip.
[*Claps a frying-pan over his head, and rides off*

SCENE II.—*A Country Road.* TURPIN *appears,*
R. H.—*Music.*

Tur. Hurrah! The limits of two shires are already past, and we shall accomplish it yet. Hall, cot, tree, river, glade, mead, waste, and woodland are seen, passed, left behind, and vanished as in a dream. Some would call this journey fatiguing; 'tis to me pleasure. I am happy—enraptured, maddened, intoxicated as with wine. Pshaw! wine could never throw me into such a burning delirium; its choicest juices have no inspiration like this.

Sir Ranalph. (*Heard without.*) Thank you. I shall find the coach at the next village.

Tur. What, Sir Ranalph Rookwood! I would rather not meet with him. No matter, I will see him.

Sir R. (*Entering.*) What do I see? Dick Turpin, the highwayman? His capture would be worth three hundred pounds, and is of equal importance to me. Stand! (*Fires at Turpin.—Aside.*) Confusion! missed!

Tur. A miss is as good as a mile, Sir Ranalph Rookwood. I know you; we have met before. I meant not to assault you, yet you have attempted my life a second time, sir. But you are now in my power, and by hell, if you do not answer me, nothing earthly shall save you! Say, is Eleanor Mowbray still at Rookwood?

Sir R. She is.

Tur. A thousand thanks. **You are now at liberty to depart.** Good night! (*Bows him off.—A miniature coach is seen to pass at the back. The horn is heard in the distance.*) So far, so well. Luke, you must gain possession of the estates. Hark! the York mail is coming this way, and heavily laden! Bess, let's step aside, and allow it to pass.

The Mail enters, L. H.

Guard. Ah, Master Turpin, I know you. Take that, and remember the guard!   (*Fires.*)

Tur. Remember you! You may rely upon it, my fine fellow, I shall not easily forget it, so I shall leave my mark behind. Take that, and remember Turpin!

(*He fires, and hits the Guard. General consternation.*)

SCENE III.—*Stamford Inn.*

OSTLER *enters with pail,* L. H.—*Music.*

Ost. Three o'clock, and nearly daybreak. I think it's time for me to turn in and take a snooze. I have been up on my precious legs since seven yesterday. They work me too hard at this place. What with the 'osses and the stable, I'm pretty well worn to a living skeleton.

TURPIN *enters,* R. H., *hastily, on Bess.*

Tur. We have gained ground on them at last, and here, old girl, you shall recruit your strength; and, though all hell opposed us, here we will stop awhile. Ostler, quick!

Ost. Who is it calling so early?

Tur. One who will pay liberally for all he has. What have you got there?

Ost. Only a pail of water.

Tur. The very thing I want. Bring me some brandy.

Ost. Missus bean't up, but how much do you want—a quartern?

Tur. A quartern, no, a quart.

Ost. Ah! that is another thing. Wait a minute, and I will see if I can get it thee.
[*Exit* L. H.

Tur. And thou too, brave Bess, thy name shall be linked with mine, and we'll go down to posterity together. What if—no matter, better die now while I am with thee than fall into the knacker's hands. Better die with all thy honours upon thy head, than drag out thy old age at the sand cart.

OSTEN *re-enters with brandy.*

Ost. Here it be; I have brought a bottle.

Tur. That's right; now for the pail.

Ost. Why, bless me, if he arn't mixing it in the pail. They must come from that wicked place, London, where I hear they drink brandy and water by pailfuls.

Tur. Here, old wench, here's a draught for thee. (*Music. Voices heard without.*) What, my pursuers close at my heels! We must be off now, Bess.

Ost. But you have forgot to pay the reckoning.

Tur. You forgot to ask for it.   (*Gives note.*)

Ost. But I can't get change for this note now.

Tur. Damn the change; give it to your sweetheart.

Beset me, ye bloodhounds,
In rear and in van;
My foot's in the stirrup,
And catch me who can.

[*Gallops off* L. H. *Pursuers enter* R. H.
—*Music.*)

Sam. What! not here? Well, he can't be far off; we are close upon him. I say, young man, have you seen the notorious highwayman, Dick Turpin, pass this way?

Ost. What sort of a man is he?

Sam. A fine-looking fellow, like myself.

Ost. What! Had he a gold lace coat on?

Sam. Yes.

Ost. And a pair of top boots, and a black hat?

Sam. Yes.

Ost. And a curly wig?

Sam. Yes.

Ost. Then I hav'n't seen him. (*General laugh.*)
[*Exit,* L. H.

SCENE IV.—*Roadside Inn.*

Enter TURPIN, R. H.

Tur. More than half the race is run; Bess has triumphed over every difficulty. Thou matchless steed! Yet brace fast thy sinews, hold on, the goal is not yet won.

Fled past on right and left, how fast each forest,
    grove, and bower,
On right and left, fled past, each city, town, and
    tower.

RALPH the OSTLER *enters, from inn,* L. H.

Ralph. Glad to see you, Captain Turpin. Can I do anything for you?

Tur. Have you any beefsteaks in the house?

Ralph. Lord love you, the old woman won't stand it at this time, but there's a cold round; mayhap a slice of that might do—or a knuckle of ham?

Tur. Damn your knuckles! Ralph, have you any raw meat in the house?

Ralph. Raw meat! Oh, yes, there's a rare rump of beef; you can have a cut off that if you like.

Tur. (*Ungirthing his mare.*) That's the thing I want; give me that scraper and some straw.
    (*Ostler goes into the house, and returns
    with the meat; meanwhile Turpin
    scrapes his steed.*)

Tur. By moonlight, in darkness, by night or by
    day,
    Her headlong career there is nothing can
        stay,
    She cares not for distance, she knows not
        distress,
    Can you show me the courser to match with
        Black Bess?

Ralph. Here be the raw meat.

Tur. (*Rolls it round the bit of the bridle.*) She'll now go as long as there's breath in her body; she'll rattle away like a woman's tongue; and when that once begins, we all know what chance the curb has. Best to let her have it out, 'twill be over the sooner. (*Sir Ranalph and constables heard without.*) Ha! are they so close upon my heels? That road takes a turn down there, don't it? Sweeps round to the right of the plantation in the hollow?

Ost. Ay, ay, captain.

Tur. What lies between the shed?

Ost. A stiff fence, captain; a regular rasper beyond the hill's side. Steep as a house. No 'oss that was ever shod can go down it.

Tur. Indeed, we will try, though.

Ost. Come into the stable, it's your only chance; quick!

    (*They rush in as the pursuers enter,*
        R. H.—*Music.*)

Sir R. (*Thundering at the door.*) Villains, come forth. You are now fairly trapped at last. Caught like the woodcock in your own springe. We have you. Open the door, I say, and save us the trouble of forcing it. You cannot escape us now.

Ralph. (*Appearing at window above.*) What do you want, master? You're clean mistaken; there's no one here but I.

Sam. That's a jolly lie.

Sir R. We'll soon see that. Force the door.
    (*Music.—The door is forced. They rush
    in. Turpin descends from above, un-
    girths their saddles, leaps upon Black
    Bess and rides off. The characters
    enter, exclaiming, "Confusion! He
    has escaped! Ah! there he goes!"
    They go to mount, when the saddles
    turn round with them. They fall as
    the scene closes.*)

SCENE V.—*Road to York. Milestone.*

Enter TURPIN *and* BESS.

Tur. Hurrah! the turrets of York Cathedral are in view! 'Tis won—'tis won! and dear Bess, I owe it all to you! One short mile and all thy troubles will be over—don't droop, old girl, I've sworn to accomplish it, and I will, though I drag thee every step; don't fail me now, old girl—she won't go much further, and I must give it—what, give up the race when it's just won? Come, come, old girl, one short mile. I have sworn it, and I will do it—come, come!
    (*Music.—He persuasively urges her off,*
        L. H.)

Enter BARBARA LOVELL, *followed by*
    SYBIL, R. H.

Bar. All is not lost while this Eleanor is within my power. The prophecy must be fulfilled, but not by Ranalph; he shall never wed Eleanor.

Syb. Whom then shall she wed?

Bar. Sir Luke Rookwood.

Syb. Oh! recall thy speech.

Bar. It is spoken; he shall wed her.

Syb. Oh, Heaven support me!

Bar. Silly wench, be firm. He shall wed her, yet shall he wed her not; the nuptial torch shall be quenched as soon as lighted; the curse of the avenger shall fall, yet not on thee!

Syb. Mother, I understand thee not. If it must fall upon the innocent head, let it be visited on mine, not on hers! I love him—would die for him! She is young—she is unoffending. Oh! do not let her perish.

Bar. It is in vain; it shall be done at once. When the stray rook shall perch on the topmost bough, my prophecy will be fulfilled. She dead, Sybil, my child, will be Lady Rookwood! Now, then, to work my purpose!
    [*Exeunt,* L. H.

Enter BALTHAZAR, R. H.

Bal. I've had no luck to-day—not a shirt upon

the hedges, not a hen-roost left open. If things
don't mend I must turn honest, and that will be a
dreadful and shocking alternative. Ha! who
have we here?

Enter SAM, R. H.

Sam. Here's a situation! I've lost my father,
I've lost my hunter, I've lost my friends, and I've
lost my vay! (*Sees Balthazar.*) Oh, what a nice
man for a small party! Please, sir, can you direct
me the nearest vay to the vorkus?

Bal. Yes, if you will peel your skin and dub up
the browns.

Sam. Peel my skin and dub up the browns!
What do you mean?

Bal. Just this—that if you do not hand over
your money I shall blow out your brains!
                                     (*Shows pistol.*)

Sam. Vot! Do you mean to say that there
pistol is loaded?

Bal. To the muzzle.

Sam. Then I knocks under—there is my purse.
(*Giving it.*) But as my father is the constable of
the parish, and I'm his brave son, it won't do to
go back as if I had been frightened. Will you
oblige me, my dear sir, by just firing off your
pistol through the tails of my coat, and then I can
tell the folks of our parish as how Dick Turpin
did it.

Bal. With pleasure.   (*Fires.*)

Sam. Capital! Now just fire another through
my hat; will you be so good?

Bal. Happy to oblige you, sir, but I really
havn't got another.

Sam. Havn't you, by goles? Then, damn your
old jacket! refund me my purse, or I'll smash your
ugly mug into a thousand pieces with this little
switch! (*Shows a large club-stick.*) Come, fork
out, or I'll make you dance to a new tune.

Bal. (*Giving back the purse.*) There, take your
blunt; I was only in joke.
              [*Runs off, L. H., followed by Sam.*

SCENE VI.—*Interior of Hut on the Thorne
                Waste.*

Music.—Enter BALTHAZAR, L. H.

Bal. The distant bell proclaims the fourth hour
of the morning; it is time for me to kindle a fire
and rouse the sleeper; he has slumbered too long
already. (*Opens a trap-door and calls below.*) Luke,
ascend! the coast is clear, and all is in readiness.

Music.—LUKE ROOKWOOD comes up trap, C.

Luke. Is it the hour?

Bal. Ay, or I should not have disturbed myself
to call you. I suppose you'll like some refresh-
ment before you start? A stoup of Nantz will put
you in cue for the job.

Luke. Ay, give me drink. I'm chilled by the
damps of that swampy cellar in which you have
concealed me.

Bal. Here is that which shall put fresh courage
in you.

        (*He opens a cupboard, produces a keg,
              and fills a glass for Luke.*)

Luke. (*Drinks.*) This is, indeed, rare Nantz, and
puts fresh fire in one's veins. That brandy has
restored me to myself, and I am not the pulseless
lump of clay I was a moment or two back. I am
now ready to execute my plans. I must depart
ere my new-blown courage evaporates. Yet

stay, I must tarry for Turpin. I fear some new
mischance has befallen him, or he would have been
here by this. What think you, Balthazar?

Bal. Since you put it home to me, I can no longer
conceal it. Dick Turpin can do nothing for you;
he's grabbed.

Luke. Apprehended? That's unfortunate. You
must supply his place, and accompany me.

Bal. There's too much risk; it won't pay.

Luke. What sum might tempt you to undertake
the enterprise?

Bal. More than you have to offer.

Luke. Name your demand.

Bal. One hundred pounds, and I must have the
chink down.

Luke. Mercenary wretch! Would that I could do
without you. (*Takes out a bag, and counts gold.*) If
I succeed, the sum shall be doubled; are you content?

Bal. (*Eyeing the bag, which Luke replaces in his
breast.*) Yes. (*Aside.*) He has more gold than I
gave him credit for; it shall soon be mine.

Luke. Come, time flies. Let us set out at once,
and provide ourselves with arms; they are in the
cellar, and I will fetch them.

Bal. No; stay where you are.

Luke. And why?

Bal. You are weaponless, and I am armed.

Luke. What do you mean?

Bal. I mean, that I must have the money you
have placed in your vest.

Luke. Treachery! You shall not have a coin!

Bal. Damnation! if you thwart me, I'll cut the
matter shorter than you expect.
          (*Produces two pistols, and presents
                them at Luke.*)

Luke. You are a coward, as well as a villain, to
take so mean an advantage.

Bal. The error is yours, not mine. You oughtn't
to have exposed a heavily-filled purse to the eyes
of an avaricious man; flashing the gold has done
all the mischief. Dub up the cash, you're sold.

*Music.—Enter TURPIN, D. F. L. H., he fires, and
            wounds Balthazar.*

Tur. No, you are sold, not he. (*Balthazar falls.*)
You see, Sir Luke, I've kept my word, I've been
damnably put to it; but here I am—ha, ha!

Luke. I heard you were taken. I am glad to find
the report was false.

Tur. Whoever told you so told you a damned lie!
I see, by your scowling, where the information
came from. Balthazar would sell his soul to the
devil, if he only got the correct valuation.

Bal. Well, captain, I only spoke as——

Tur. Cut your blarney whids, and let's have no
more gammon, we've got more serious work on
hand than listening to it. Sir Luke, make all
haste to the hall; the Philistines are in the neigh-
bourhood, and have an inkling of your where-
abouts.

Bal. (*Aside.*) The devil! Then my little game is
clear.   (*Going.*)

Tur. (*Detaining him.*) No you don't; in business affairs, I always communicate with my asso-
ciates myself. By the way, it won't be amiss if I
drop you a line. (*Takes out a cord and throws it
over Balthazar's head.*) Nothing like a binding
contract in these cases. (*Tightens the noose round
Balthazar's body.*) Lead the way, Sir Luke; pass
through the garden at the rear of the house, we
shall more readily escape observation. (*To Bal.*

thazar.) Come along, my tulip; to prevent mischief you shall accompany us. Yo, ho!

[*Pulls Balthazar off with the rope—the prisoner receives cuffs, Luke follows them out. After a pause, SIMON and SAM SHARPSCENT enter.*

Sam. Tut, tut, father, I tell you we are on the right scent. I've received credible information, this is one of the ruffian's haunts, and if you will use a little patience you'll see how I'll bag my game.

Sim. But mayhap the rogue will be making game of us.

Sam. No, no! leave me alone for that! I've taken my measures.

Sim. Yes, very likely for a coffin; that Dick Turpin *sticks* at nothing, and it might be very inconvenient if he took it into his head to *stick* at us.

Sam. Father, you want pluck, you require spirit.

Sim. By gosh, you're right there, son; I'd just like a taste of brandy, if it was only to keep out the fog.

Sam. Well, I don't think a modicum of the fluid would do us any harm, seeing that we've been travelling from London since yesterday morning. Here, house——

Enter TURPIN, R. H., *disguised as a countryman, in a smock frock, shock wig, and squint eyes.*

Eh, who are you?
Tur. (*With a strong country dialect.*) Thought 'ee called for house.
Sim. So I did.
Tur. Well, I be the house—He, he, he!
Sim. Bring us some *eau de vie.*
Tur. Eau de vie; He, he, he!—who be he?
Sim. Brandy, you blockhead.
Tur. Oh, ha! He, he, he!—there be some in the cupboard. Master keeps it for his special drinking.

(*Music.—Turpin brings on table and chairs, R. H.,—the others take off their overcoats, and lay their pistols on table. Turpin brings brandy-bottle and glasses. Sam and Simon drink.*)
Sim. Excellent. I'll be sworn the strength was never tested by a gauger's proof. Son, what is your opinion of the liquor?
Sam. Are you asking medicinally?
Sim. As a professional man, not as a parent, I ask your opinion of this brandy.
Sam. My opinion, then, of brandy is this:—

SONG.—SAM.

A drop of good brandy's the best thing in life,
Tol de rol, &c.,
To make up a quarrel, or comfort a wife;
Tol de rol,
It warms a cold heart, and it fires a dull train,
And makes a sad dog a good fellow again.
Tol de rol.

All know 'tis a pleasure when brandy they touch,
Tol de rol,
But some drink too little, and some drink too much,
Tol de rol,

If it gets to your head, you've no use of your legs,
Tol de rol,
So, remember, there's reason in roasting of eggs,
Tol de rol.

(*During the above song Turpin has poured brandy down the pistols on the table, and rendered them useless; this action has been unobserved by Simon and Sam Sharpscent.*)
Sam. Come, chawbacon, let me hear what you have to say.
Tur. He, he—I were thinking that my *bacon* face and thy *calf's* head would make a capital dish.
Sim. By gosh! but a *stupid* yokel is sometimes a man of *sense.*
Sam. Are you aware that I am a person of consequence?
Tur. Be thee, though? La, I should never thought it, thee looks such a fool. He, he, he!
Sam. No reflections on my personal appearance. Now, hark ye, fellow; we're in search of a notorious character. In fact, I want to put my hand upon Dick Turpin.

(*Puts his hand on Turpin.*)
Tur. Dick Turpin! Eh, eh, folks do say that talking of him is like speaking of the devil; he's at your elbow when you mention his name.
Sam. Here's a description. (*Glances over a paper he takes from his pocket, and then looks at Turpin.*) Bless me, what a resemblance! (*Reads.*) "Age: about thirty." How old are you, young man?
Tur. Well, he, he, I were twenty-nine when feyther's pig died.
Sam. Well, we'll dispense with your father's pig, and proceed. (*Reads.*) "About five-foot nine inches."
Tur. Just my height, barring the inches.
Sam. (*Reads.*) "Of prepossessing appearance."
Tur. Yes, my Betty says, I be a main pretty lad.
Sam. Now, I appeal to you, father, does not all this sound like a portrait of Turpin?
Sim. Oh, don't appeal to me! I don't want to have anything more to do with the blackguard! I can hardly sit down through him!
Sam. I wish I had the opportunity. At the present moment, I'd take him, dead or alive!
Tur. Would you, indeed? Then make good your words, for I am Dick Turpin!
Sam: Ha, ha!—the pistols! Father, guard the door! Surrender, or I fire!
Tur. Blaze away! (*The pistols of Simon and Sam hang fire.*) Ha, ha! your weapons have had a drop of *eau de vie!* Attempt to follow me, and you die on the spot!

(*Fires his pistols in the air. Sam falls, and Simon jumps about in alarm.*)

SCENE VII.—*Gipsy Barn on the Common. The Spires of York Cathedral seen in the distance. Bess discovered, dead; TURPIN by her side, c.—Music.*

Tur. And art thou gone, Bess? Gone—gone! And I have killed the best steed that was ever crossed; and for what—for what? (*Bell chimes.*) I am answered. It was to hear those sounds—

"O'er highway and byeway, in rough or smooth weather,
Some thousands of miles have we journeyed together;
Our couch the same straw, our meals the same mess;
No couple more constant than I and Black Bess!"

Luke. (*Advancing,* R. H.) So it's all over with the best mare in England. I see—I can guess how it happened. You are pursued?

Tur. I am.

Luke. They are at hand?

Tur. Within a few hundred yards.

Luke. Then why stay here? Fly while you can!

Tur. Never—never! I'll fight it out here, by Bess's side! Poor lass! I have killed her, but she has done it! Ha, ha! we have done it!

(*Falls convulsively across Bess.*)

Luke. Hark! I hear the tramp of horses! Take this wallet—you'll find a change of dress within it. Dart into yonder copse, and summon our tribe. Save yourself!

Tur. And Bess—I cannot leave her?

Luke. And what did Bess die for, but to save you?

Tur. True, true; but take care of her—don't let those dogs of hell meddle with her.

Luke. Away—leave Bess to me.

Tur. Mark me—if ever I am brought to Tyburn Tree, I can never feel half so smart a pang as I do now at parting from thee, thou matchless steed!

(*Dives into the wood,* L. U. E.—*Music.*— *Pursuers enter,* R. H., *headed by* SIR RANALPH ROOKWOOD.)

Ran. (*Seizing the gipsy.*) This is not Turpin.

Luke. I am not exactly the figure for a highway-man. This dead horse, lying in the road, attracted my attention.

Ran. This vain subterfuge will not avail; doubt-less he is concealed by the gipsy tribe. Search yonder barn.

Luke. (*Guarding the door.*) You pass not here!

Ran. We'll see that. Force the door!

Luke. (*Blowing a shrill whistle.*) Upon him, lads!

(*Music.—Gipsies rush out. General scuffle, in the midst of which* BAR-BARA *drags forwards* ELEANOR. *The hag draws a pistol, and fires at her.* SYBIL *enters at the moment, and receives the ball intended for Eleanor, and falls into the arms of Luke Rook-wood. Eleanor rushes across to Sir Ranalph, who protects her from the fury of Barbara. Turpin protects the body of Black Bess with a brace of pistols. The constables are over-powered. The burning barn lights up the effective concluding tableau.*)

CURTAIN.

---

www.ingramcontent.com/pod-product-compliance
Lightning Source LLC
Chambersburg PA
CBHW081456070426
42452CB00042B/2756